Please visit our website, www.enslow.com. For a free color catalog of all our high-quality books, call toll free 1-800-398-2504 or fax 1-877-980-4454.

Library of Congress Cataloging-in-Publication Data
Names: Lombardo, Jennifer, author.
Title: The story of bigfoot / Jennifer Lombardo.
Description: New York, NY : Gareth Stevens Publishing, [2023] | Series: Monster madness | Includes index.
Identifiers: LCCN 2021059960 | ISBN 9781978531666 (library binding) | ISBN 9781978531642 (paperback) | ISBN 9781978531659 (set) | ISBN 9781978531673 (ebook)
Subjects: LCSH: Sasquatch–Juvenile literature.
Classification: LCC QL89.2.S2 L647 2023 | DDC 001.944–dc23/eng/20211217
LC record available at https://lccn.loc.gov/2021059960

Published in 2023 by
Enslow Publishing
29 E. 21st Street
New York, NY 10010

Copyright © 2023 Enslow Publishing

Designer: Tanya Dellaccio
Editor: Jennifer Lombardo

Photo credits: cover (illustration) Shutterstock.com; pp. 5 (plaster feet), 15 (photos) John Zada/Alamy Images; p. 5 (sign) Teri Virbickis/Shutterstock.com; p. 7 Dale O'Dell/Alamy Images; p. 9 Cavan Images/Alamy Images; p. 11 (footprint) Igor Shoshin/Shutterstock.com; p. 11 (forest) Alex Stemmers/Shutterstock.com; p. 13 Photo 12/Alamy Images; p. 15 (illustration) CPYstudio/Shutterstock.com; p. 17 https://upload.wikimedia.org/wikipedia/commons/3/33/Eric_Shipton_yeti_footprint.png; p. 19 (bears) PhotocechCZ/Shutterstock.com; p. 19 (paw print) Maksim Semin/Shutterstock.com; p. 21 (crossing sign) Dennis Swena/Shutterstock.com; p. 21 (Bigfoot area sign) CineBlade/Shutterstock.com.

All rights reserved. No part of this book may be reproduced in any form without permission in writing from the publisher, except by a reviewer.

Printed in the United States of America

Some of the images in this book illustrate individuals who are models. The depictions do not imply actual situations or events.

CPSIA compliance information: Batch #CSENS23: For further information contact Enslow Publishing, New York, New York, at 1-800-398-2504.

CONTENTS

MANY NAMES, ONE CREATURE. 4

SHARING THE STORIES 8

TRICKING PEOPLE 10

A FAMOUS VIDEO 12

REAL OR FAKE? 14

SASQUATCH IN THE SNOW. 16

JUST A MYTH?. 20

GLOSSARY. 22

FOR MORE INFORMATION 23

INDEX 24

Boldface words appear in the glossary.

MANY NAMES, ONE CREATURE

People say a monster lives in the woods. It's huge and hairy, with red eyes. Reports say it's between 6 and 15 feet (1.8 and 4.6 m) tall! They say it looks like a cross between a person and an ape. Because it's so big, its footprints are also huge. This is where it gets the name Bigfoot.

Bigfoot is often also called Sasquatch. This name comes from the word "Sasq'ets," which means "wild man" or "hairy man" in the Salish language. Salish is spoken by the Salish First Nations people.

THESE MODELS OF BIGFOOT TRACKS WERE MADE BY POURING **PLASTER** INTO A FOOTPRINT ON THE GROUND AND WAITING FOR IT TO HARDEN.

BIG FOOT XING

DUE TO SIGHTINGS IN THE AREA OF A CREATURE RESEMBLING "BIG FOOT" THIS SIGN HAS BEEN POSTED FOR YOUR SAFETY

BELIEVE IT OR NOT!

BIGFOOT'S MAIN **HABITAT** IS THE NORTHWEST PART OF THE UNITED STATES AND CANADA. OUT OF ALL THE U.S. STATES, WASHINGTON HAS THE MOST REPORTED SIGHTINGS. HOWEVER, PEOPLE HAVE REPORTED BIGFOOT SIGHTINGS IN EVERY STATE EXCEPT HAWAII!

Native American groups have known about Bigfoot for a long time. In fact, there are more than 50 names for the creature! Many Native American groups believe it has special powers, such as the ability to move between the **physical** world and the spirit world. This means it might only visit our world instead of living here.

Some say it has **psychic** powers that let it play tricks on people's minds and can make itself **invisible** whenever it wants. This might explain why it's so hard to find!

BELIEVE IT OR NOT!

MANY PEOPLE WALKING THROUGH THE WOODS HAVE REPORTED HEARING THE SOUND OF A STICK HITTING A HOLLOW LOG OR HAVING ROCKS THROWN AT THEM. THE GREAT LAKES INDIANS SAY THIS IS HOW YOU CAN TELL YOU'RE IN SASQUATCH **TERRITORY**.

IT'S ILLEGAL IN CANADA TO KILL A SASQUATCH—IF YOU CAN FIND ONE!

SHARING THE STORIES

A man named J. W. Burns talked to Sts'ailes Salish people and wrote down their stories of Sasq'ets sightings. In 1929, these stories appeared in *Maclean's* magazine. This was the first time white people were hearing about Sasquatch, and they thought it was a joke.

Most white people forgot about Sasquatch until the 1950s. That's when René Dahinden and John Green started separately looking for **evidence**, such as footprints and hair. Other people soon became interested in the hunt as well. Some people say they have taken photos and videos of Bigfoot.

BELIEVE IT OR NOT!

MOST PEOPLE WHO BELIEVE BIGFOOT EXISTS SAY THERE ISN'T JUST ONE BIGFOOT. PEOPLE HAVE TOLD STORIES ABOUT IT FOR HUNDREDS OF YEARS, AND MOST CREATURES DON'T LIVE THAT LONG. THERE MIGHT BE WHOLE BIGFOOT FAMILIES OUT THERE SOMEWHERE!

STS'AILES TERRITORY

THE STS'AILES PEOPLE ARE NATIVES OF BRITISH COLUMBIA, CANADA.

TRICKING PEOPLE

In 1958, a newspaper reporter wrote about a trail of huge footprints that was found in California. That was the start of Bigfoot's popularity. However, most of the evidence has turned out to be fake.

In 2002, after a man named Ray L. Wallace died, his children told everyone he had made the prints in 1958 with feet carved out of wood. Other people have played jokes like this over the years. In 2008, two men said they had found a Bigfoot's body. They later told everyone that they had lied.

SOME PEOPLE THINK THE BIGFOOT PRINTS THAT HAVE BEEN FOUND BELONG TO HUMANS OR OTHER ANIMALS.

BELIEVE IT OR NOT!

NO ONE HAS EVER BEEN ABLE TO PROVE THAT BIGFOOT EXISTS. SOME SCIENTISTS HAVE DONE TESTS ON HAIR AND TEETH THAT HAVE BEEN FOUND IN THE WOODS. THEY TURNED OUT TO BE FROM ANIMALS SUCH AS BEARS, PORCUPINES, DOGS, AND SHEEP.

A FAMOUS VIDEO

In 1967, Bob Gimlin and Roger Patterson went out to look for Bigfoot in northern California—and they found one! They took a video of her. That video is now called the Patterson-Gimlin video, and it's the clearest evidence of Bigfoot that exists, even today.

A lot of people say the video proves for sure that Bigfoot is real. However, just as many people say the video was a **hoax**. They think the video shows a person in a costume. No one knows for sure what the truth is.

BELIEVE IT OR NOT!

THE MOVIE *PLANET OF THE APES* CAME OUT IN 1968. MANY PEOPLE THINK THE BIGFOOT IN THE PATTERSON-GIMLIN VIDEO IS WEARING A COSTUME LIKE THAT. OTHERS SAY THE COSTUMES LOOK TOO FAKE TO FOOL ANYONE. WHAT DO YOU THINK?

DO YOU THINK A MONKEY COSTUME LIKE THESE WOULD TRICK SOMEONE?

PLANET OF THE APES MOVIE

REAL OR FAKE?

Bob Gimlin and Roger Patterson have always said their video was real. Many people have watched the video over and over to see if it's true. Some are trying to see if Bigfoot walks like a human. Others are trying to decide if the creature looks like a person in a costume.

In the 1980s, a costume maker named Philip Morris said he had sold Patterson a costume. In 1999, a man named Bob Heironomous said he wore the suit. Bob Gimlin says they're lying because they want money. No one knows for sure who's right.

IMAGES FROM THE PATTERSON-GIMLIN VIDEO

350 352 364

MOST DRAWINGS OF BIGFOOT LOOK LIKE THIS. THE POSE COMES FROM THE PATTERSON-GIMLIN VIDEO.

BELIEVE IT OR NOT!

MORRIS AND HEIRONOMOUS CAN'T PROVE THEY'RE TELLING THE TRUTH BECAUSE NEITHER OF THEM HAVE THE SUIT. THEY BOTH **DESCRIBE** IT DIFFERENTLY. SOME PEOPLE THINK IT'S BEEN SO LONG THAT THEY JUST FORGOT SOME THINGS. OTHERS SAY THEY'RE LYING.

SASQUATCH IN THE SNOW

Many other countries have stories of a creature like Bigfoot. One of the most famous is called the Yeti. In the Sherpa language, this means "wild man." The Yeti lives in the mountains of Tibet and Nepal. As far back as 326 BCE, tales were told of a huge, humanlike monster in the Himalayas, a mountain range in that area.

In 1951, a British man named Eric Shipton was looking for a new way to the top of Mount Everest when he found a human-looking footprint in the snow. He took a photo to prove it.

BELIEVE IT OR NOT!

IN INDONESIA, PEOPLE TALK ABOUT THE ORANG PENDEK, WHICH MEANS "SHORT MAN" IN MALAY AND INDONESIAN. LIKE BIGFOOT, IT'S A CROSS BETWEEN A HUMAN AND AN APE, BUT IT'S SHORTER THAN A HUMAN. HOWEVER, IT'S ALSO SAID TO HAVE INCREDIBLE STRENGTH.

STORIES ABOUT HUGE, HUMANLIKE MONSTERS CAN BE FOUND IN MANY OTHER PLACES AROUND THE WORLD.

FOOTPRINT PHOTOGRAPHED BY ERIC SHIPTON

NAME	LANGUAGE/COUNTRY
YEREN	CHINESE / CHINA
BIGFOOT	ENGLISH / UNITED STATES
YOWIE	KÁMILARÓI / AUSTRALIA
ALMAS	MONGOLIAN / MONGOLIA
SASQ'ET (SASQUATCH)	SALISH / CANADA
YETI	SHERPA / NEPAL
BARMANOU	URDU / PAKISTAN

People got very excited about the Yeti footprint. Yeti hunting became so popular that the U.S. **embassy** in Nepal gave out a list of rules in 1959. It said that people had to buy Yeti-hunting **permits** for $77. They could only kill a Yeti if they were in danger, and they had to give the government of Nepal any photographs they took of the creature.

However, the Yeti turned out to be a **myth**. In 2017, scientists tested Yeti hair and found that it all came from bears.

BELIEVE IT OR NOT!

THE HIMALAYAN BROWN BEAR SOMETIMES WALKS ON ITS BACK LEGS. IF A PERSON SAW IT DOING THIS, THEY MIGHT THINK IT WAS A HUMANLIKE CREATURE, ESPECIALLY IF THEY COULDN'T SEE IT WELL. BEAR FOOTPRINTS ALSO LOOK A LOT LIKE HUMAN FOOTPRINTS.

JUST A MYTH?

Many people believe Bigfoot is a myth just like the Yeti. They say we would have found Bigfoot bodies or bones by now, just like we find the bodies of other animals that die in the woods. They also think it's silly to believe a group of creatures could be so good at hiding.

People also say it's strange that there are no good photos or videos of Bigfoot. Cameras have gotten a lot better since 1967, but all the pictures people take seem to turn out blurry.

MANY PEOPLE THINK BEARS ARE MISTAKEN FOR BIGFOOT ALL THE TIME.

BELIEVE IT OR NOT!

MAKING A PHOTO OR VIDEO BLURRY IS A GOOD WAY TO KEEP PEOPLE FROM FINDING OUT IT'S FAKE. FOR EXAMPLE, IF A PERSON IS WEARING A COSTUME WITH A ZIPPER IN THE BACK, A BLURRY PHOTO WOULD MAKE IT HARD TO SEE THE ZIPPER.

GLOSSARY

describe: To write or tell about.

embassy: A group of people who represent their country in a foreign country.

evidence: Something that helps show or disprove the truth of something.

habitat: The natural place where an animal or plant lives.

hoax: An act meant to trick someone into believing something that is not true.

invisible: Unable to be seen.

myth: Like a legend or story.

permit: A printed document from a government or organization that allows someone to own or do something.

physical: Having to do with things that can be experienced with the five senses.

plaster: A wet paste that hardens when it becomes dry.

psychic: Having supernatural abilities to affect a person's mind.

territory: An area of land that an animal considers to be its own and will fight to defend.

FOR MORE INFORMATION

BOOKS

Besel, Jennifer M. *Bigfoot*. Mankato, MN: Black Rabbit Books, 2020.

Gish, Ashley. *Bigfoot*. Mankato, MN: Creative Education, 2020.

Oachs, Emily Rose. *Bigfoot*. Minneapolis, MN: Bellwether Media, 2019.

WEBSITES

CBC Radio: "Cowboy behind legendary Patterson-Gimlin Bigfoot film marks 50th anniversary"
www.cbc.ca/radio/asithappens/as-it-happens-wednesday-edition-1.4360203/cowboy-behind-legendary-patterson-gimlin-bigfoot-film-marks-50th-anniversary-1.4362363
In 2017, CBC Radio talked to Bob Gimlin about the famous Bigfoot video.
This article includes the video itself.

Myths and Folklore Wiki: Yowie
mythus.fandom.com/wiki/Yowie
Learn more about Australia's Yowie.

Publisher's note to educators and parents: Our editors have carefully reviewed these websites to ensure that they are suitable for students. Many websites change frequently, however, and we cannot guarantee that a site's future contents will continue to meet our high standards of quality and educational value. Be advised that students should be closely supervised whenever they access the internet.

INDEX

bears, 11, 18, 19, 21

Canada, 5, 7, 9, 17

costumes, 12, 13, 14, 21

footprints, 5, 8, 10, 16, 18, 19

Gimlin, Bob, 12, 14

Himalayas, 16

hoaxes, 10, 12, 13, 14, 15

Native Americans
  Great Lakes, 6
  Salish, 4, 8, 17

Nepal, 16, 18

Patterson, Roger, 12, 14

Patterson-Gimlin video,
  12, 13, 15

Sasquatch, 4, 6, 7, 8, 17

United States, 5, 17

videos, 8, 12, 13, 14, 15,
  20, 21

Wallace, Ray L., 10

Yeti, 16, 17, 18, 19, 20